SNOOPY

Books by Charles M. Schulz

Weekly Reader Children's Book Club presents

A NEW *PEANUTS* BOOK

FEATURING

SNOOPY

by Charles M. Schulz

HOLT, RINEHART AND WINSTON
New York • Chicago • San Francisco

Published, August, 1958

In Canada, Holt, Rinehart and Winston
of Canada, Limited

Copyright © 1955, 1956, 1957, 1958 by United Feature Syndicate, Inc.
Printed in the United States of America
All rights reserved
Library of Congress Catalog Card Number: 58-9353

ISBN: 0–03–029930–6

LISTEN TO THIS DEFINITION IN THE DICTIONARY..

"dog (dog) I. n 1. Domestic quadruped. 2. Andiron. II vt. Follow as a dog."

OH, HO HO HO HO HO!! A DOMESTIC QUADRUPED! WOW! AN ANDIRON! HA HA HA HA!

I MIGHT AS WELL GO HOME AND GO TO BED..THIS COULD TURN OUT TO BE A VERY BAD DAY...

EMPTY WATER DISH!

SCHULZ

SCHULZ

REMEMBER THE ALAMO!!

MMMMMMMMM

COOL BREEZE

SCHULZ

AND SOMETIMES WHEN A DOG ISN'T FEELING WELL, YOU'LL SEE HIM EATING GRASS.

BLAHH!!

SCHULZ

ZIP!

I JUST CAN'T TURN DOWN A BEGGING DOG..

SCHULZ

WHERE ARE THOSE MARBLES?

I **DEMAND** TO KNOW WHO TOOK THOSE MARBLES!

I JUST BETTER NOT CATCH THE GUY WHO'S GOT THOSE MARBLES!

SCHULZ

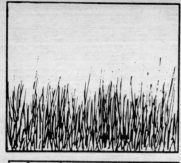

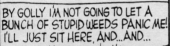

AHCHOO!

THE FLOOD WATERS ARE RISING!!

SCHULZ

SCHULZ

EXCUSE ME.. I THINK SOMEBODY'S WATER DISH IS EMPTY

SNOOPY, I'VE GOT SOMETHING TO SAY TO YOU!

NOW, YOU SIT DOWN, AND LISTEN TO ME!

YOU SIT HERE, AND LISTEN TO WHAT I HAVE TO SAY!

AND DON'T ROLL UP YOUR EARS!!

GOOD GRIEF! I THINK I
FROZE MY STOMACH!

STUPID DOG!

FLOODS, FIRE AND FAMINE!

DOOM, DEFEAT AND DESPAIR!

I GUESS ITS NO USE.. ✳ SIGH ✳

NOTHING SEEMS TO DISTURB HIM!

I'VE HEARD THAT A LOT OF CROOKS HAVE TINY EYES...

OH, THAT'S TRUE...YOU CAN'T TRUST ANYONE WHO HAS SMALL EYES...

LET'S SEE **YOUR** EYES, SNOOPY...

SCHULZ

HE'S RIGHT... I **DO** HAVE A FUZZY FACE!

MMM!

I LIKE YOU, SNOOPY... I LIKE YOU BECAUSE YOU HAVE SUCH A WARM, FUZZY FACE!

PEANUT BUTTER!

HE LOVES PEOPLE!

"UP PERISCOPE!"

WHY CAN'T YOU JUST COME TROTTING UP LIKE OTHER DOGS?

I GOTTA START LEARNING SOME NEW STEPS..

SCHULZ

THE WORST THING A PERSON CAN DO IS WASTE HIS LIFE HANGING AROUND STREET CORNERS!

SCHULZ

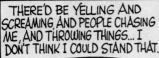